Countdown
to Christmas

Countdown to Christmas

Ryan and Adrienne Nuñez

NCP
NEW CITY PRESS
Enkindling the Spirit of Unity

Published in the United States by New City Press
136 Madison Avenue, Floors 5 & 6, PMB #4290
New York, NY 10016
www.newcitypress.com

Cover Design: Gerrod Martinez

ISBN: 978-1-56548-635-5 (Paperback)
ISBN: 978-1-56548-640-9 (E-book)

Library of Congress Control Number: 2024945389

Printed in the United States of America

Contents

Introduction

Like many people, Christmas has always been our favorite time of the year. Our whole lives become immersed in the season, with Christmas music coming from every source and Christmas-themed shows on television. The stores are decorated, our homes are decorated, and knickknacks that would never see the light of day under normal circumstances are proudly displayed on our shelves because they have a Christmas theme.

This amazing time between Thanksgiving and Christmas Day seems to fly by each year. This whirlwind is partially because it's a fun season, and as they say, time flies when you are having fun. But it also seems to pass quickly because of all the preparations that need to be made. There are so many things to do because we want Christmas Day to be perfect: the perfect meal, the perfect gifts, the perfect tree, the perfect decorations. It needs to be just right!

We have four kids, and for the first few years of parenting, we really struggled with balance at Christmas time. We had this incredible desire to make the season magical. We wanted it to be memorable for them and us, and yet, with each added activity and event during the season, we also felt like we were losing the true meaning of Christmas. Don't get me wrong; we were not ignoring the fact that Christmas was the celebration of Jesus' birth. We talked about Christmas being Jesus' birthday, and our church did a great job teaching our kids and providing great opportunities for family discussions. But it honestly felt like we were straddling two different paths each Christmas. We had one foot solidly on the traditionally commercial Christmas path and the other on the celebration of the birth of Jesus. They weren't conflicting—they were just different. And if we were honest with ourselves, Jesus wasn't getting the attention he deserved.

Then came our breakthrough. After a few years of frustration and regret, we decided to put Jesus back at the center of our Christmas season. What helped us do this was choosing to celebrate Advent as a family. Now, for many Christians around the world, this is as natural as Santa Clause is to the United States, but in our Christian tradition, we never used the word Advent or celebrated anything like it in the weeks leading up to Christmas.

For centuries, Christians have celebrated the weeks leading up to Christmas as a time of expectation and waiting. Advent simply means arrival. It is a season of expectation for the arrival of the birth of Christ, a countdown to Christmas that focuses on Jesus.

So, we started a new tradition. Each day leading up to Christmas, our family sits down and reads a small devotional that tells the story of the coming birth of Jesus. The whole Bible points in expectation to the birth of the Savior, so we start with the creation of the world and walk through the Scriptures right up to his birth. This family devotional time has become the foundation and rhythm of our season for the past few years. It is a short five-to-ten-minute time each day that allows our family to refocus on what the season is about.

We want to be clear that we do not think the other Christmas traditions are bad. In fact, we're not proposing that we remove any of them. We still decorate for Christmas, put lights on the house, and purchase gifts. We have a very traditional Christmas celebration, but at the foundation of it all is a countdown through Scripture to the arrival, or advent, of Jesus.

By shifting the focus of our preparations for Christmas to the person of Christ, we bring new depth and joy to our Christmas celebration. We also join with Christians around the world in unity as we take this journey. Although our cultures vary in how we celebrate Christmas, our faith unites us as we focus on Jesus.

The *Countdown to Christmas* book contains the readings we developed as we put this new tradition into practice. We invite you to take the journey with us this Christmas, whether you are taking it alone, with your family, or with some friends. We pray that this Christmas season is more Jesus-focused than the last.

Merry Christmas!
Ryan and Adrienne Nuñez

How To Use This Book

The *Countdown to Christmas* is designed to be read by individuals or as a family. The book is divided by date. You simply read each day's selection on the assigned day, beginning on December 1 and ending on December 25, Christmas Day.

Each day has a few questions that can be used for personal reflection or discussion with your family or group.

Making It Fun

Let's get real for a minute. When we started celebrating the countdown to Christmas that first year, we had a picture in our minds of how it would be. It went a little like this: at the end of each day, we would lovingly call our children to come to the living room for our devotional. Our kids would come the first time they were called and quietly sit on the floor, eagerly waiting for that day's story. They would watch and listen with rapt attention, clinging to every word that was said. (We think we can feel the eye-rolls now as you read this). Well, maybe that is a bit of an exaggeration, but you get the idea. We had very high expectations.

We sometimes have unrealistic expectations of our children and their attention spans. For this endeavor to succeed, we would need to make this tradition attractive to our kids. We wanted our children to LOVE this time we spent focusing on the coming Savior. There was only one thing to do—we needed to raise the "fun factor." To accomplish this, we decided to integrate some of the things we loved about Christmas and make them part of our countdown to Christmas tradition. We encourage you to consider what your family enjoys at Christmas and to be creative about integrating those activities into your daily countdown to Christmas time. Here are some of the things we do that may help you to get your creative juices flowing.

Make a Special Snack

Our family loves food. Two of the things we love about Christmastime are the amazing desserts and seasonal beverages you can either make or buy at your local coffee shop. A warm plate of chocolate chip cookies can pretty much get our kids to do anything. So, we started making a special treat to accompany our countdown to Christmas time. Some nights it would be cookies, sometimes cinnamon rolls, sometimes popcorn, but it was always special, something that we didn't have all the time. Hot chocolate is usually the drink of choice for our family, so we have it readily available, with a cute Christmas mug for each person. We have to tell you, our kids love it.

The "Countdown to Christmas" Tree

Like many families, we have moved to a pre-lit Christmas tree that we decorate the day after Thanksgiving. It is a fun day that we can spend with our kids, making our tree as gaudy as possible. But growing up, we always enjoyed the smell of fresh pine in the house, so as we were building our countdown to Christmas tradition, we decided to add to it a smaller, fresh Christmas tree. We call this tree our "Countdown to Christmas" tree. It sits in our living room right next to where we do our devotionals. We string a set of lights on this tree, and at the beginning of December, we begin to decorate it. Each night during our family devotional, one of the kids adds an ornament to the tree that symbolizes that evening's story. By the end of December, the tree is decorated with ornaments that tell a story of the coming Savior.

An added activity, should you want one, is making ornaments that coincide with each story. The sky is the limit with something like this and you can let your imagination run wild. If you are not the crafty type, you can purchase a set of ornaments and write a number on each one for the countdown to Christmas. Kids do well with interactive activities, and ours really love this part of our tradition.

The Surprise Chocolate

Another "fun factor" in our countdown to Christmas tradition is the use of an Advent calendar. At the beginning of the season, we buy each of the kids a chocolate-filled calendar that has a little door for each day. You have probably seen them in the stores at Christmastime. Our kids love this little treat, and at the end of our devotionals, each of the kids is allowed that day's chocolate. It is very simple but something they look forward to every night.

I am sure there are many other ideas that you and your family will dream up, but these are just a few activities we use to make our time special. We hope you truly enjoy this journey you are about to take with your family and that it is as big of a blessing to you as it has been to us.

In the Beginning

In the Bible are four books that we call the Gospels, or Good News: Matthew, Mark, Luke, and John. They each tell the account of the life of Christ. Over the next twenty-five days, we will be reading selections from each of these books as well as many other passages from the Bible.

Each Gospel author begins his account at different starting points. Mark begins with Jesus at the age of about thirty. Matthew and Luke begin with the birth of Jesus. John, however, takes us back to the beginning of the universe.

As we start this countdown to Christmas, we need to be mindful of the fact that Jesus did not come into existence on that first Christmas morning. Jesus has always existed.

> In the beginning the Word already existed.
> The Word was with God,
>   and the Word was God.
> He existed in the beginning with God.
> God created everything through him,
>   and nothing was created except
>   through him.

> The Word gave life to everything that
>   was created, and his life brought light
>   to everyone.
> The light shines in the darkness,
>   and the darkness can never extinguish it.
> So, the Word became human and made his
>   home among us. He was full of unfailing
>   love and faithfulness. And we have seen
>   his glory, the glory of the Father's one
>   and only Son.
> (John 1:1-5, 14)

John begins his gospel account by making sure that the reader understands that Jesus is God. This fact is central to all that we believe as Christians. If Jesus were not God, then his mission on earth would be empty. Jesus came down to earth to rescue mankind from their sins. Jesus proved he was God by conquering death and rising from the dead on the third day. But let's not get too far ahead here; that's another holiday.

What we celebrate on Christmas is the day God became man. He took on flesh and bones. Jesus was 100 percent God and 100 percent man. If you are good with numbers, you probably realize that the math on that does not add up. That is why it's a mystery. No one can fully grasp this attribute of God. The fact that I cannot fully understand

intimate relationship for a peer relationship. God was the creator, and they were his creation. To demonstrate this, God gave them a rule—a boundary. He was in charge, and they were not. The rule revolved around a tree at the center of the garden, called the Tree of the Knowledge of Good and Evil. They were commanded to never eat from this tree, or they would surely die.

Those were very clear expectations. Everything in the entire garden, except one thing, was available to them. Enjoy the garden, enjoy creation, enjoy our time together—but if you choose to disobey me by eating from this one specific tree, you will die.

Even if you have never heard this story before, you probably know where it's headed. Adam and Eve ate the fruit of the tree. Satan entered the garden and tempted them with a lie. Lies are Satan's specialty. He said that they would not die if they ate from the tree, but that they would become like God, knowing everything.

Adam and Eve gave into the temptation and broke God's rule. Because of this, sin entered the world. This broken rule fractured the relationship between God and man because God is perfect and holy and cannot associate with sin. Man chose sin over God. Man rebelled. The consequence was death, not only a physical death that would now be the curse of all creation but also a deeper death than that—a spiritual death, a separation from God.

It is important to understand that there is the direction of the rebellion. God did not walk away from man. No, man chose to separate from God by choosing death. When we watch the news, we often wonder how a good God could allow such evil things to happen. God did not. We did. Man chose sin and death over a good and loving God.

The story of man would be a very short one if it were not for one thing—God's love. Man rejected God, but because of God's love for man, he made a promise and gave us hope. As Adam and Eve were leaving the garden, God promised to conquer death. There was no timeline given. There was not an immediate remedy or description of what this would look like. There was only hope. This promise is found in the curse God delivers to the serpent, Satan. "And I will cause hostility between you and the woman, and between your offspring and her offspring. He will strike your head, and you will strike his heel." (Gen 3:15)

Christmas is the ultimate fulfillment of this promise. God chose to conquer death by sending the Savior down to earth to pay the penalty for man's sin and conquer death. In the first chapters of Genesis, we don't know the fullness of God's plan; however, we have a promise that one of Eve's offspring will one day defeat the serpent. As we travel through the Scriptures, we will see God unfold this plan with more clear and focused promises and messages to his people through the prophets about what to look for.

This promise gives us hope, and hope leads to expectation. As we journey through these passages this Christmas season, we are counting down to the coming of the Savior.

Reflection Questions

1. Why do you think God repeatedly declared his creation as "good" throughout the poem of creation in the Bible? What might this indicate about his perspective on creation and his relationship with it?

2. How do you think Adam and Eve's ability to choose impacted their relationship with God and their eventual decision to disobey him?

3. In the story of Adam and Eve, why do you think they chose to disobey God's command even though they had clear expectations and were given so much else to enjoy? What lessons can we learn from their decision and its consequences?

Christmas Connection

God's promise to save man from the consequences of sin will become clearer as we get closer to Christmas. Today, we see the first hint of this promise as God delivers his curse to the Serpent, whom we know as Satan. He says one of the woman's offspring will "strike your head, and you will strike his heel." This refers to Jesus coming to earth to defeat Satan. As we count down to Christmas, we are counting down to the fulfillment of this promise.

Noah and the Ark

What is more impressive, renovating a broken-down home back into its original state or building a new house from scratch? Both are difficult, but restoration takes a bit more effort because you are working around other people's mistakes. The restoration takes love and commitment. Sometimes in a restoration project, you have to take a building back to the bare bones, but you do it because you are committed to the original structure—it was good in the beginning, and it can be good again.

God is a God of Restoration

Adam and Eve are obedient to God's command to be fruitful and multiply. They have babies. These babies grow up to have babies of their own. After many years, the region is becoming populated with people. The problem is that these people are separated from God by sin.

When Adam and Eve rebelled against God, the effect of sin in the world was devastating. Sin always destroys. Sin is the exact opposite of God's desires for us and his world. Sin spreads and escalates. This separation from God and rebellion against his desires had a catastrophic effect on man and the world God had created.

God's thoughts on the state of affairs are recorded in Genesis: "The Lord observed the extent of human wickedness on the earth, and he saw that everything they thought or imagined was consistently and totally evil. So, the Lord was sorry he had ever made them and put them on the earth. *It broke his heart.*" (Gen 6:5-6)

God's initial response to this sin explosion on earth is to destroy it. Man has chosen to live apart from his creator and is causing pain and suffering for all of creation. God could have ended it all, but he had made a promise. God promised that a descendant of Eve would defeat Satan, and God always keeps his promises.

God saw one righteous man down on earth named Noah, whom he chose to preserve. God was going to send a flood to destroy mankind, but he chose to preserve Noah and his family to rebuild and fulfill his promise.

Noah and his family, along with two of every animal, were all protected in the ark that God instructed Noah to build. After about a year inside the ark, Noah and his family walked out into a renewed earth. Sin was not eliminated with the flood because Noah and his family were a product of the fallen world, but the flood was a fresh start, a new beginning for man.

As they exited the ark, God made a promise to Noah and all his descendants: He would never again destroy the earth by flood. The symbol of this promise is the rainbow. Whenever we see a rainbow, we are reminded of God's promise and his preservation of man.

God's promise to rescue man from sin continues to develop through the account of Noah. The Savior is coming! We wait with expectation to see how God will reveal his plan and timing.

Reflection Questions

1. Why do you think God chose Noah to preserve and start again after the flood?

2. How does the story of Noah and the flood show God's commitment to giving humanity a fresh start? Can you think of other examples of restoration in your own experiences?

Christmas Connection

God always keeps his promises. He promised that he would send the Savior who would be a descendant of Eve. He kept his promise by saving Noah and his family, descendants of Eve, so that Jesus could be born someday.

God's Promise to Abraham

There are moments in some people's lives that are so significant, so transformational, that we would say they are a different person afterwards. That's the case of the person we are looking at today. God asked a man named Abram to do something so significant that he changed his name after the encounter. He started off as Abram but became Abraham. For most people, that's the name we are more familiar with. So, for the purpose of today's account, we are just going to call him Abraham.

Abraham was living a great life. He was living in the land of Ur, which was the greatest city of his time. It was full of people, opportunity, and excitement. His family was successful, and he was on the pathway to even greater success. But all of this was about to change when God asked Abraham to take a big step of faith.

> The Lord said to Abram, "Leave your native country, your relatives, and your father's family, and go to the land which I will show you. I will make you into a great nation. I will bless

you and make you famous, and you will be a blessing to others. I will bless those who bless you and curse those who treat you with contempt. All the families on earth will be blessed through you." (Gen 12:1-3)

A simple definition of faith is to trust or believe someone, without proof or evidence. I think that definition fits perfectly with this situation. God is asking Abraham to leave everything he knows for the unknown—the literal unknown—God didn't even tell him the name of the place where he was being sent. The God that Abraham has never met, never seen, and until now had never heard from is asking Abraham to trust him.

God's plan is not to send Abraham on some wild goose chase. The step of faith God is asking Abraham to take comes with a reward. There are three promises that God makes. The first is that the land he is sending him to will be his. He will own it and can pass it down to his future descendants. The second is that his descendants will become a great nation. He is going to have a really big family. The third promise is that through this family or nation, the whole world will be blessed. His family will have a positive global impact.

What God is doing is making a covenant with Abraham. A covenant is an agreement between two parties; if you meet certain conditions, then you will receive the agreed-to benefits.

This promise or covenant between God and Abraham further clarifies God's redemptive plan. The picture is becoming clearer. In the Garden of Eden, God promised that one day a descendant of Eve would defeat the curse of sin. God is narrowing down the people he is going to use to defeat sin. It's not just any family on earth that he is going to work through; he is going to use Abraham's family, the Israelites.

As we said before, this step of faith was such a giant leap that it changed Abraham's entire identity. He left his homeland and his family ties. His destiny was changing so much that a change of name was given. Abram (which means high father) was now to be known as Abraham (father to multitudes).

Reflection Questions

1. How do you think Abraham felt when God asked him to leave everything behind and go to a place he didn't even know? What would be the hardest part about obeying God's command in this situation?

2. Why do you think God made such big promises to Abraham when he asked him to take this step of faith? How do you think these promises helped Abraham trust in God's plan?

3. Can you think of a time in your life when you had to trust someone or something without having all the evidence or proof?

Christmas Connection

Part of the promise that God made to Abraham was that the whole world would be a better place because of him and his family. God said, "All the families on earth will be blessed through you." This blessing is Jesus. God was going to use Abraham's big family to bring Jesus into the world.

Abraham and Isaac

As we continue in the story, remember that God made a promise to Abraham that he would create a great nation through his offspring and the entire world would be blessed through him. Abraham and Sarah did as they were asked and moved to a far-off land that God showed them. The problem was they were very old. In fact, they were past the age of having children.

Seeing this problem, Abraham and Sarah chose to seek a solution in Abraham taking another wife and having a child through that union. This was not the promise God made to Abraham and Sarah. They are reminded that the promise will be fulfilled through a child brought through Sarah. God did not need assistance in fulfilling the promise he had made.

Finally, Abraham (age one hundred) and Sarah (age ninety) welcomed a son named Isaac. Abraham loved Isaac very much. He now had a son who would carry on his name, to whom he could pass along his possessions, and a son who fulfilled the promise God had made so many years ago. It was a slow start; one child was a far cry from a "nation," but at least there was a chance. But let's see what happens next:

Some time later, God tested Abraham's faith. "Abraham!" God called. "Yes," he replied. "Here I am."

"Take your son, your only son—yes, Isaac, whom you love so much—and go to the land of Moriah. Go and sacrifice him as a burnt offering on one of the mountains, which I will show you." (Gen 22:1-2)

Now that is an unexpected request, to say the least. God wants to know if Abraham loves him more than he loves his son, Isaac. Is the God that Abraham has never seen with his eyes more real to him than his son who holds all his hopes for the future? Perhaps that's the point. Now that Isaac is in the picture and will carry on the family name, does Abraham still need God?

Why does Abraham need another test of faith? Didn't he already show his faithfulness by moving to the new land and leaving everything behind? Of course, this *is* another test, but it's also more than that. It is a picture of something else to come.

As we wait with bated breath, we find out Abraham is obedient and has complete faith in God. He takes his son to the mountain to make a sacrifice. Isaac is a bright and observant child who notices that they are not taking an animal along with them. They have the wood and the fire, but no sacrifice. Abraham responds to Isaac's questions with the faith-filled statement: "God will provide a sheep for the burnt offering, my son." (Gen 22:8) God would provide the sacrifice.

Abraham goes far along in the process of sacrificing Isaac. He builds the altar, ties up Isaac, and lays him on the altar, and then raises a knife to kill him before God stops him. "Don't lay a hand on the boy!" the angel said. "Do not hurt him in any way, for now I know that you truly fear God. You have not withheld from me even your son, your only son." (Gen 22:12)

Abraham looks up to find a ram caught in a brush nearby. God had provided a sacrifice.

This image of God providing the sacrifice is a snapshot of what God is going to do in the future through the Savior. In fact, one of the most important verses in the Gospels points directly back to this account of Abraham and Isaac.

In John, chapter three, Jesus has this amazing encounter with a man named Nicodemus. He had some questions about Jesus, his mission, and how he himself could have eternal life. The conversation goes back and forth a while when Jesus says one of his most quoted verses: "For this is how God loved the world: He gave his one and only Son, so that everyone who believes in him will not perish but have eternal life." (John 3:16)

It is hard to miss the similarity in the phrasing of this verse compared to the passage where God asks Abraham to sacrifice his son, his only son, on the altar. John, the author of this Gospel, connects these two scenes with this intentional language. The sacrifice of Isaac and the sacrifice of Jesus are meant to be connected.

God gave his Son Jesus to this world for a specific reason—not just to do miracles or teach important lessons, but to be a sacrifice. God's plan of redemption involves a sacrifice.

We are now one step closer; the image of what God is doing is a little bit sharper.

Reflection Questions

1. Why did God ask Abraham to sacrifice his son, Isaac? Do you think it was a difficult test for Abraham?

2. Abraham had already shown his faithfulness by moving to a new land, so why do you think God needed to test him again? What do you think this test symbolizes?

3. How does the story of Abraham and Isaac connect to the message Jesus shared in John, chapter three, about God giving his one and only Son? What similarities do you see between these two stories?

Christmas Connection

God tested Abraham's faith again because God wanted to know if Abraham really trusted him with everything. This also is a picture of God's promise. We cannot imagine someone giving up their only son. We cannot imagine it because of the love a father has for his child. But this kind of sacrifice is exactly what God is going to do. God is going to send his Son Jesus down on earth as a sacrifice for our sin. God loves his Son like any father would. He also loves us. He loves us so much he is willing to send his Son Jesus down on earth to save man from sin.

Jacob and Esau

God chooses all kinds of people to bring about his promise of sending the Savior. Some of them are what we might expect: spiritual, faith-filled saints. But more often than not God uses people with some pretty big flaws. Today, we are introduced to a man named Jacob. He fits into the character flaw category for sure. He is a liar, a thief, a cheat, and a swindler. Yet despite this, God uses him to accomplish his purpose.

Jacob is the grandson of Abraham and the son of Isaac. He has a twin brother who is older by just a few minutes. By being born a few moments after his brother Esau, Jacob lost out on the larger portion of his father's inheritance, as well as all the other social benefits that come from being the first-born son. To make matters worse, Jacob's parents have picked favorites. Jacob is a mama's boy, and Esau is his father's favorite. This is truly a family with a lot of conflict, as we can see in the following consequential interaction between the two brothers.

Esau, after working hard outside all day, comes into the family home extremely hungry. He is so hungry that he is not thinking straight about anything.

Jacob decides to take advantage of the situation and offers to give his brother something to eat in exchange for his birthright, or inheritance. Foolishly, Esau agrees to the price, and the deal is struck.

This situation tells us quite a bit about each brother's character. Jacob is obviously a manipulator; however, Esau does not value his position in the family or hold it with much care. To make matters worse, later on, Jacob tricks his old, blind father by pretending to be Esau, thereby stealing a blessing meant for his older brother.

This is the tipping point for Esau, and he is going to have it out with Jacob. That's actually a nice way of putting it; Esau wants to kill Jacob. Jacob has taken everything from him. Wisely, Jacob chooses to flee the land to escape his brother's anger.

Even though trickery and manipulation ruled the day, a legitimate transfer of the birthright had taken place. There was an agreed upon exchange that took place between Jacob and Esau. For all intents and purposes, Jacob was now the first-born son of Isaac. With this came the inheritance, leadership in the family, and the promise that God had made to Abraham.

Because so many sketchy things had occurred, God made an appearance to Jacob as he was fleeing his brother to confirm that he was going to keep his promise through him. That night as Jacob slept under the open night sky with a rock as a pillow, he had a dream. In the dream was a staircase leading to heaven with angels traveling up and down. Then God spoke in an audible voice.

> I am the Lord, the God of your grandfather Abraham, and the God of your father, Isaac. The ground you are lying on belongs to you. I am giving it to you and your descendants. Your descendants will be as numerous as the dust of the earth! They will spread out in all directions—to the west and the east, to the north and the south. And all the families of the earth will be blessed through you and your descendants. What's more, I am with you, and I will protect you wherever you go. One day I will bring you back to this land. I will not leave you until I have finished giving you everything I have promised you. (Gen 28:13-15)

During the most confusing and scary moment of Jacob's life, God shows up. Even though Jacob's troubles are the result of his own choices, God does not abandon him. God's promise is still intact. Despite the errors and failures of members of Abraham's family, God continues his faithfulness. He will send a Savior through the line of Abraham, Isaac, and Jacob. The land that God had promised Abraham will continue to be Jacob's despite the fact that he is fleeing his homeland for his life.

Reflection Questions

1. Why do you think God chose Jacob, despite his flaws, to be a part of his plan to send the Savior? Do you think it's important for us to remember that even people with flaws can be used by God for important purposes?

2. When Jacob had his dream of the staircase to heaven and heard God's promises, how do you think that affected his outlook on his situation? Have you ever had a moment when you felt scared or confused, but then something happened to make you feel reassured or hopeful?

Christmas Connection

Despite Jacob's flaws, he is still part of God's plan to send the Savior. God made a promise to Abraham that he would make a great nation from him. Abraham and his wife Sarah had one son named Isaac. Isaac then had two sons, Jacob and Esau. This family is not growing very fast, but God made a promise, and he always keeps his promises. God reconfirms his promise to send a Savior to Jacob and lets him know that it is through his descendants that his promise will be fulfilled.

While hiding from his brother in a foreign land, Jacob got married and had twelve sons. It took him many years to come back home and seek forgiveness and restoration with his brother Esau. When he did, God changed his name from Jacob to Israel. Jacob's twelve sons became the twelve tribes of Israel. As we count down to Christmas, we are waiting for the birth of Jesus who will be born from the house of Israel.

Joseph in Egypt

As the countdown to the arrival of the Savior continues, let's examine the family tree of Abraham and see where it takes us. Abraham had one son with his wife Sarah. Isaac had two sons Jacob and Esau. The birthing of the nation that God had promised was slow in the beginning. Jacob, however, really gets things moving with the addition of twelve sons.

Jacob's twelve sons and their families eventually become the twelve tribes of Israel. Jacob is given a new name by God, and that name is Israel. God created a nation from this one big family, just as he had promised. However, before we go too far down the road, let's focus on Jacob's most famous son, Joseph.

Joseph was Jacob's second-youngest son and his favorite. We know this because Jacob broke the cardinal rule of parenting and showed favoritism toward Joseph. Jacob reserved the best clothes and the best jobs for him. This quickly led to jealousy in the house of Jacob, and for the next few years, Joseph is run through the ringer.

Tensions among the brothers were high, and Joseph pushed his brothers too far when he told them that he had had a dream where they all bowed down to him. As a result, Joseph's brothers sell him into slavery, and he is taken to Egypt. During this time, Joseph honors and serves whoever is placed over him. The situations he finds himself in are difficult; for instance, Joseph works in the home of an Egyptian whose wife lies about him. Consequently, Joseph is sent to prison because of that betrayal. Through every one of these experiences, Joseph's character remains intact.

Eventually, Joseph is given an incredible opportunity. While in prison, Joseph becomes known for his ability to interpret dreams. One of the prisoners whom he helped by interpreting a dream was ultimately restored to Pharaoh's court. So, when Pharaoh has a dream that no one could translate, this man remembers his experience, and Joseph is called upon to help.

The meaning of Pharoah's dream was very simple: There would be seven years of great harvests followed by seven years of famine. Because of Joseph's incredible insight and reputation, Pharaoh asks him to be his second-in-command to organize the storage of surplus grain and supplies in the years of plenty so they could make it through the famine.

Joseph once again exceeded expectations, with the help of God. Egypt was the only land that thrived through the regional famine. In fact, Egypt did so well that people from surrounding nations came to Egypt for assistance during this devastating time. One of the families that reached out for help was the house of Israel.

The house of Israel was on the brink of starvation, with no chance of survival unless they could get some assistance from the land of Egypt. Joseph's brothers made the long journey to Egypt for supplies, without any knowledge of their brother's well-being. They had long assumed that he had died or had been traded to a distant land. They did not think that they would ever see him again. Little did they know what God had been doing to preserve them.

After several trips back and forth and interactions with Joseph, whom they did not recognize, Joseph finally reveals his identity to his brothers. Much to their shock, he is not vindictive. He was not after revenge at all. In fact, Joseph understood what God was doing all this time. "You intended to harm me, but God intended it all for good. He brought me to this position so I could save the lives of many people." (Gen 50:20)

God was at work keeping his promise to Abraham. Through his descendants would come the Savior. He would go to any length to preserve the house of Israel. Even if it meant sending a brother away for a period of time to make preparations.

Reflection Questions

1. How did Joseph's brothers feel about him, and what actions did they take because of their feelings? How did Joseph's character remain strong even in challenging situations like being sold into slavery and being falsely accused?

2. When Joseph revealed his identity to his brothers, why were they shocked, and how did Joseph react to them? What did Joseph understand about God's plan through all the difficulties he faced?

3. How did Joseph play a crucial role in preserving his family during the famine?

Christmas Connection

God continues to provide for his people in unusual ways, and God always keeps his promise. God could not have his people die in a famine, so he used the selfish actions of Joseph's brothers to ultimately save them. As long as the family of Israel survives, God is keeping his promise, and they continue to have hope that the Savior is coming.

DECEMBER 8

Moses and the Burning Bush

The Israelites have now been in Egypt for four hundred years. A new Pharaoh has come to power who does not know about Joseph and his efforts to save Egypt from the famine. The family of Israel, who were once the honored guests of the kingdom, are now slaves.

Moses was born at a unique time, during this captivity in Egypt. The Pharaoh was concerned that the population of Israelites was growing too strong to manage, so he set a policy in place where all the newborn baby boys were to be killed. Moses escaped this fate through a miracle.

Moses' mother placed him in a water-sealed basket and put the basket in the river to hide him. Pharoah's daughter, while bathing in the river, discovers Moses floating among the reeds. She takes him in and raises him as her own child. Moses, the Israelite, was now a prince of Egypt.

Even though he was raised in Pharaoh's palace, Moses never forgot his heritage. He knew that he was an Israelite and felt a burden for his people. This emotion wasn't always managed well. It came out as anger one day when he saw an Egyptian taskmaster beating an Israelite slave. Moses intervened and beat the taskmaster to death. Despite his attempts to cover up the crime, word got out, and Moses fled into exile.

It is during this exile that we find Moses tending sheep. He has married into the family of a man named Jethro and has started a new life. His position in life had drastically changed from a Prince of Egypt with power, authority, and comfort, to a nomadic shepherd. Moses's life had taken a dramatic turn. It would have been hard for him not to dwell on his mistakes and regrets while roaming alone in the vast desert landscapes.

Day after day, for years on end, Moses cared for his sheep, with each day being almost the same as the previous one. Until one day, off in the distance, Moses spots a fire. As he approaches the scene, he realizes that this is no regular fire. The bush at the center of the flame is not burning up. In fact, as Moses gets closer, a voice speaks out: "Moses, Moses!"

> "I am the God of your father—the God of Abraham, the God of Isaac, and the God of Jacob." When Moses heard this, he covered his face because he was afraid to look at God. Then the Lord told him, "I have certainly seen the oppression of my people in Egypt. I have heard their cries of distress because of their

harsh slave drivers. Yes, I am aware of their suffering. So I have come down to rescue them from the power of the Egyptians and lead them out of Egypt into their own fertile and spacious land. It is a land flowing with milk and honey—the land where the Canaanites, Hittites, Amorites, Perizzites, Hivites, and Jebusites now live. Look! The cry of the people of Israel has reached me, and I have seen how harshly the Egyptians abuse them. Now go, for I am sending you to Pharaoh. You must lead my people Israel out of Egypt."

(Exod 3:6-10)

God had not forgotten his promise over all these years. He promised Abraham a land, a people, and a Savior. The suffering of his people has not escaped him. It was now time to bring his people back into their promised land, and God was asking Moses to lead them.

Despite God showing up in a flame and speaking to him in an audible voice, Moses still had his doubts. He had a credibility issue back in Egypt because of the murder he committed, and he struggled with public speaking because of a voice impediment.

God's response was profound. He told Moses his name: "I Am." Yes, the personal verb that indicates existence. This is not an easy name to communicate to those who ask. But what name could reflect the power and majesty of the creator of the universe? "Frank" is just not going to cut it. Not only did he tell Moses his name; he told Moses that he would be with him—every step of the way.

God had made a promise to his people and the world. A pharaoh in Egypt was not going to stand in the way. God was going to use Moses to bring about his plan.

Reflection Questions

1. How do you think growing up as a prince in Egypt and then living as a shepherd in exile shaped Moses's character and prepared him for the task God had for him? Can you think of any experiences in your own life that have helped you grow or prepare for challenges?

2. When Moses saw the burning bush and heard God speaking to him, why do you think he was afraid? How do you think he felt when God told him about his plan to rescue the Israelites from slavery?

3. Even though Moses had doubts and struggles, why do you think God chose him to lead the Israelites out of Egypt? What qualities or characteristics do you think made Moses a good leader, despite his flaws? Can you think of any examples of leaders in your own life who have overcome challenges to lead others?

Christmas Connection

The Israelites have been living in Egypt since Joseph brought his family there to take care of them. During that time, two major things happened: the family grew to over one million people, and the Israelites became the Egyptians' slaves. God never forgets his promises. God promised Abraham a great nation in the land he gave him, and that the entire world would be blessed by the Savior. Promise one has been fulfilled; they were a great nation. To fulfill the rest of his promises, God needed to get them back to the land he promised Abraham. Moses was one of the people God used to bring about his plan of sending the Savior. One more step forward in the countdown to Christmas.

Passover

There are many events in the Scriptures that fore-shadow what God is going to do in the future. The Israelites are being held as captives in Egypt. They are bound in slavery and not experiencing the promises that God made to their forefather Abraham. But God has not forgotten them and is sending Moses to lead them out of captivity into the promised land. This event is called the Exodus and is a picture of what God is going to do for all mankind when he sends the Savior.

Let's think for a moment how difficult it would be to free one million slaves. It would be impossible to slip away undetected at night, under the cover of darkness. Considering the number of people, and the complexities of a strategic plan of that size, we can assume the communication of such a plan, without any Egyptian officials discovering it, would be highly unlikely. As a result, the plan Moses settles on is relatively simple. Moses will meet with Pharaoh and tell him to let the people go. After all, the creator of the universe, who controls all creation, is on their side. He has the power to do whatever he wants, so why should his people sneak away in the middle of the night or bolt for the border when the guard is down?

Moses initially approaches Pharaoh with this very request and is quickly dismissed. Letting an entire workforce walk away in the middle of his projects was not something Pharaoh was willing to do. Why should he anyway? He was the most powerful man in the world. He does not give in to demands; other people give in to his demands. Moses receives his answer: a resounding "No".

This was not a shock to Moses, and certainly not to God. Moses knew Pharaoh would need some convincing that God, the great I Am, is not like the gods of Egypt. The God of Israel was real and powerful and would make himself known to them all.

Pharaoh's response triggered a series of plagues unleashed on the people of Egypt: the Nile River turned to blood, frogs invaded the land, a gnat infestation, thick swarms of flies, the death of Egyptian livestock, a plague of festering boils, destructive hail, locusts, and darkness over the land. After each plague, Pharaoh asked for mercy and promised to let the people go. Once the plague was lifted, Pharoah would deny the request, which ushered in the next plague. Pharaoh's hard heart persisted, and as Egyptians suffered through these plagues, God spared the Israelites.

The final plague would prove to be the most devastating and would lead to the Israelite's release. This plague would cause the death of every firstborn male, both human and animal. From Pharaoh's palace to the lowest of slaves, no one would escape this terrible judgment.

God made a provision for his people to spare them from this final plague, by giving very specific instructions through Moses. On the specified evening, each Israelite family would prepare a special meal. They would bake bread without yeast or leavening agents and eat the roasted meat of a young goat or lamb. The people would eat this meal while fully clothed, with sandals on and a walking stick in hand. This was a meal on the go. They were headed on a journey back to the promised land.

As a sign that they were following God's instructions, they were to take some of the blood from the lamb or young goat and spread it over the doorposts of their home. This blood of the sacrifice showed that they were under God's protection, and death would pass over their home. The firstborn son would be spared, and the family would be preserved and saved for the exodus that was to come.

As we continue to follow the story of God's redemption plan for man, it is becoming clearer what he is going to do. A sacrifice for man is at the center of God's plan. We don't know the details yet, and we don't know exactly what this is going to look like at this point, but we see a foreshadowing in this event. Because of the blood of the lamb, God passed over the Israelite households.

The celebration of Passover was a feast that God commanded his people to celebrate each year. This was not because he was going to wipe out the firstborn sons every year; it was because he wanted his people to remember this day. God wanted this event to be engrained in his people's lives, to be remembered and celebrated each year.

As we quickly fast-forward in time, we find Jesus celebrating Passover with his disciples on the night he was to be betrayed and turned over for death. The passage says:

> Now the Festival of Unleavened Bread arrived, when the Passover lamb is sacrificed. Jesus sent Peter and John ahead and said, "Go and prepare the Passover meal, so we can eat it together."
>
> He took some bread and gave thanks to God for it. Then he broke it in pieces and gave it to the disciples, saying, "This is my body, which is given for you. Do this in remembrance of me."

After supper he took another cup of wine and said, "This cup is the new covenant between God and his people—an agreement confirmed with my blood, which is poured out as a sacrifice for you. (Luke 22:7-8, 19-20)

We see a snapshot of what is to come. God is revealing his plan for a Savior in the exodus of his people from slavery, just as he will someday rescue all mankind from the slavery of sin.

Reflection Questions

1. Think about the story of the Passover when the Israelites were saved from slavery. What do you think the blood on the doorposts symbolized, and why was it important to have God's protection?

2. Why do you think God asked the Israelites to celebrate Passover every year? How did Jesus continue this idea during the Last Supper, and why is it important for us to remember his sacrifice today?

Christmas Connection

God is rescuing his people from the bondage of slavery in Egypt just like he is going to rescue everyone from the bondage of sin when he sends the Savior. Passover, as this night came to be known, was celebrated every year by the Israelites. It was a constant reminder of their rescue by God from Pharaoh, but also a picture of the future rescue from sin. When the Savior arrived, God would provide a way through his sacrifice to pass over our sin.

The Ten Commandments

Most people are familiar with the Ten Commandments. We don't necessarily have them memorized or have a printout somewhere in our homes as a checklist for doing the right thing, but most people have a general awareness of the fact that these rules have existed for a very long time and have served as a basis for how humans should behave. These foundational laws serve as a basis for most Western cultures even to this day.

When God gave the Ten Commandments to his people, it was a further clarification of his promise. In fact, for the first time, there were some explicit terms in his covenant. The covenant he made with Abraham and confirmed with Isaac and Jacob promises that he would create a great nation from their offspring and that through their heirs he would send the Savior. The law God was now giving them served as the terms or conditions of this covenant.

Through the miraculous acts of God, Moses led the people out of Egypt and on toward the promised land of Canaan. This was the land God had given to Abraham who then passed it on to Isaac, who passed it on to Jacob, who then had to leave it because of a famine. And now, they were on their way back. A great nation had been formed out of Jacob's (Israel's) twelve sons, just as God had promised. Moses was now leading the twelve tribes of Israel who now numbered about one million people.

While camped at the base of Mt. Sinai, God calls Moses up onto the mountain. It was there that he delivered to him the Ten Commandments written on stone tablets. In Exodus, chapter twenty, we find the Ten Commandments. They can be summarized as follows:

> You must not have any other god but Me.
> You must not make or worship an idol of
>   any kind.
> You must not misuse the name of the Lord
>   your God.
> Remember to observe the Sabbath day by
>   keeping it holy.
> Honor your father and mother.
> You must not murder.
> You must not commit adultery.
> You must not steal.
> You must not testify falsely against your
>   neighbor.
> You must not covet your neighbor.

God did not expect that the people would be perfect from this point on. He knew that the nature of man was bent toward sin. Sin means to disobey God's commands and desires. The big question that hung out there was this: What do I do when I mess up? Is it game over, end of story, God's done with you? How is God ever going to deliver on his promise if no one can follow his rules perfectly? The solution was the sacrificial system.

God is a loving God and desires community with his people. He is also perfect and holy and cannot associate with sin. We are sinful people. We break his rules and create a divide between God and us. If we are to have a relationship with God, sin needs to be removed from our lives. The problem is that there is nothing we can do to remove sin. Good deeds don't erase bad deeds. In fact, one of the other attributes of God that comes into play here is that he also has a perfect sense of justice. He cannot let sin go unpunished. A penalty must be paid for sin.

The Savior will ultimately pay the penalty for sin when God sends him. Until then, God set up the sacrificial system for his people. When they broke one of God's commands, they needed to go to the house of worship and make a sacrifice in order to pay that penalty.

This sounds very ritualistic, and in many ways it was. There were many guidelines and specific ways that these sacrifices were to be made. If it wasn't done exactly right, God would not accept the sacrifice. However, at the center of this system was a deep and necessary component of personal faith. Faith was placed in the future hope that God was sending a Savior. Each individual sacrifice was an act of faith that God would forgive. Each sacrifice was also a picture of how God would make one final sacrifice, a perfect one, by coming down on earth himself to pay the penalty for all of mankind's sin.

All forgiveness is through faith. We do not earn God's forgiveness. During the time of the sacrificial system, it was a faith that looked forward to the cross. During our time it is a faith that looks back at the cross. It has always been about faith.

> If his good deeds had made him acceptable to God, he would have had something to boast about. But that was not God's way. For the Scriptures tell us, "Abraham believed God, and God counted him as righteous because of his faith." (Rom 4:2-3)

Abraham believed God's promise and acted accordingly, by faith. It wasn't his deeds and actions that made him right before God; it was his faith. The same is true today. However, the difference is we look back in time at what the Savior did verses looking forward to the promise of what the Savior will do.

Reflection Questions

1. Why do you think God gave the Ten Commandments to his people?

2. How do you think the sacrificial system helped the Israelites understand forgiveness and their relationship with God?

3. How does the idea of faith play a role in understanding forgiveness and following God's commands?

Christmas Connection

The reason that God promised the Savior to us was because of our sin. Sin separates us from God. Because God loves us, he chose to solve our sin problem by sending Jesus to pay the penalty for our sin. The coming Savior, Jesus Christ, will be the final sacrifice. Through his death, he will pay the penalty for all of mankind's sin.

The Day of Atonement

God's desire is for all men and women to be in relationship with him. This is why he gave his people rules to live by. He also gave them a way to reconcile the errors they made, also called sin, which is what separates man from God. This was called the sacrificial system. When a person broke a law or command, they had to go to the temple to make a sacrifice in order to pay the penalty for that sin. It was in this way that man could maintain a relationship with God.

This system was for more than just individual sin management. God looked at his people as a whole community. There were things that they did collectively that displeased him and broke his commands; therefore, he wanted them to come together collectively to seek forgiveness. This was done annually on what was known as the Day of Atonement. This day is another picture or snapshot of God's ultimate redemptive plan. It is a snapshot of the promised Savior.

On the Day of Atonement, after making a sacrifice for his own personal sins, the high priest would present two goats to the people. The first goat would be sacrificed as a sin offering. The blood of this goat would be taken into the holy of holies. This is that place where the ark of the covenant is held. The ark of the covenant was the vessel that God had the Israelites create to contain the Ten Commandments and Aaron's staff. The actual presence of God was in this place. It is the only time of the year when the priest was allowed to enter into God's presence. There he placed the blood as an offering for the people's sins.

Upon returning from the holy of holies, the high priest presented the second goat to the people. There he placed his hands on the goat and began to confess all the people's sins onto it. At that moment, the sins of the nation were placed onto this goat. This goat, however, was not killed, it was led out from the city into the wilderness to wander. The goat that was sent out was called the scapegoat, and even though this goat had done no wrong, it was burdened with the task of carrying the people's sins. This was the visual representation of their sins being taken away, never to return again. The sins of the people were removed from them because of the forgiveness of God and the sin offering of the first goat.

After the sacrifice of the first goat and the sending of the scapegoat, a celebration took place. The Day of Atonement marked the beginning of a new year. God had given his people a fresh start, and the sins of the past no longer lived with them. This sentiment is reflected in Psalm 103, verse 12: "He has removed our sins as far from us as the east is from the west."

Every new year another goat would be sacrificed, and another goat would be sent out of town carrying the sins of the camp. This would continue to happen until God sent the Savior. As we are discovering through his plan, the Savior would be the final sacrifice. The Savior would be the perfect sacrifice that would not need to be repeated each year.

The Scriptures are the inspired Word of God. We use them as our source for understanding God's plans and desires for our lives. Aside from the Bible, there are many other writings that support the teaching of Scripture. We do not take them with the same weight and reliability as the Bible, but they are often helpful in filling in some of the historical information. One of these writings is the Jewish Talmud. It is essentially the writings of Jewish rabbis.

An interesting detail that the Talmud adds to the Day of Atonement is that a scarlet cord was tied around the neck of the scapegoat to differentiate it from the goat that was to be sacrificed. This cord was then removed from the goat before it was led away from the city and hung in a place for all to see. Each year a miracle would occur where the scarlet cord would turn white. This represented the people's sins being taken away. In fact, the prophet Isaiah uses language that reflects that this tradition may be accurate. "Come now, let's settle this," says the Lord. "Though your sins are like scarlet, I will make them as white as snow. Though they are red like crimson, I will make them as white as wool." (Isa 1:18) Once again, this ties into the big picture of what God is going to do through the Savior. But it gets even better. As you continue to read through the writings of the Talmud, an interesting fact is recorded about the Day of Atonement. The rabbis taught that forty years prior to the destruction of the temple, the lot did not come up in the [high priest's] right hand nor did the tongue of scarlet wool become white. (Babylonian Talmud, Tractate Yoma 39b)

The destruction of the temple was in AD 70, meaning that from AD 30 onward, the scarlet cord stopped turning white. This is significant because the death of Jesus, according to many Bible scholars, occurred at this time. Jesus had made the final sacrifice for mankind's sin. The previous agreement or covenant God had made with man was now replaced because of Jesus' sacrifice. The cord no longer turned white because the scapegoat was no longer needed.

Reflections Question

1. On the Day of Atonement, what were the roles of the two goats, and what did each symbolize?

2. How did the Day of Atonement mark a fresh start for the people each year, and why was there a celebration afterward?

3. How does the scarlet cord in the Talmud story connect to the idea of sins being forgiven and the ultimate sacrifice made by Jesus according to the Bible?

Christmas Connection

Sin separates us from God. If there was something that we could do to get rid of our sin, God would just have told us and left the problem for us to solve. The truth is that only God can forgive sin and that is why he promised to send a Savior. This promise was fulfilled with the birth of Jesus.

Rahab and the Spies

God's promise to Abraham was a nation, a land, and a Savior. The nation was up and running but they were not in the promised land yet.

It had been about four hundred years since Jacob and his family left the land of Canaan for Egypt to escape a deadly famine. During this time, many different groups of people had moved in. These groups of people apparently liked the land and did not want to leave. For the Israelites, entering the promised land was not just simply moving into a new home, they had to remove the current occupants.

God had done some amazing miracles for his people as he rescued them from Egypt; he parted the Red Sea, provided food from heaven, made clean water appear from rocks, and defeated military threats. Despite this, they did not think God would help them remove a few squatters from their land. This lack of faith displeased God so much that he sent them back out into the desert for another forty years until every adult from that doubting generation, except Joshua and Caleb who had faith, was dead.

As the Israelites approached the promised land for the second time, they did so with a different mindset. They were going to trust God this time. As they made their preparations, they chose to send in a few spies to scout out the land. The spies entered the town of Jericho, which was the first town they would need to conquer on their path to reinhabiting their promised land.

The spies entered the city of Jericho and ended up in the home of a prostitute named Rahab. Word was spreading quickly that the Israelites were headed toward them and that there were spies in the city. A search was quickly organized throughout the town. Rahab put her life on the line and took the spies and hid them from the city officials. Later that evening she went up to the roof where they were hiding. The Book of Joshua states:

> "I know the Lord has given you this land," she told them. "We are all afraid of you. Everyone in the land is living in terror. For we have heard how the Lord made a dry path for you through the Red Sea when you left Egypt. . . . No wonder our hearts have melted in fear! No one has the courage to fight after hearing such things. For the Lord your God is the supreme God of the heavens above and the earth below. (Josh 2:9-11)

Rahab wanted to be on the winning side of this fight, and she knew without a doubt which side that would be. Although she didn't know him, she believed that the God of the Israelites was powerful and real. She wanted to be on his side. They came to a very simple agreement; during the attack, she was to hang a scarlet cord out of her window. The Israelite men would be given instructions that whoever was in this home was to be spared. They would spare her life as she had spared and protected theirs.

Reflection Questions

1. Why do you think Rahab decided to help the Israelite spies, even though it put her own life at risk? Can you think of a time when you had to make a difficult choice to help someone, even though it might have been risky or scary?

2. How does Rahab's story show that God's plan of redemption is for everyone, not just a specific group of people?

Christmas Connection

Although Rahab was not an Israelite, she could see God's power and wanted to be on his side. After the destruction of Jericho, she joined the Israelite community and started a new family. She joined the story of God's rescue plan. God was sending a Savior to the world through the Israelites and now she was a part of that same family. In fact, as we continue to count down to Christmas, we will see that it is one of her direct descendants, Mary, who gives birth to Jesus.

Ruth and Boaz

The theme of redemption comes up over and over again in the lives of God's people. It's sending signals that this is the big thing that God is going to do.

The Merriam-Webster's Dictionary defines the word redeem as "to buy back." I love this definition, as it relates to God's plan for us. It is because of mankind's rebellion that we are separated from God. We cannot pay the penalty for our own sin, so God chose to solve the problem by sending his Son to pay the penalty. God is redeeming us from death, by settling sin's penalty with Jesus' life.

Today we look at a snapshot in God's redemptive history. The Israelites are now settled in the promised land. Two parts of God's promise have been fulfilled; there is a nation, and they are in the promised land. Now they await the Savior.

Elimelech and Naomi had two sons, Mahlon and Kilion, and they were from the town of Bethlehem. A famine broke out in the land, and Elimelech chose to move his family from the promised land to Moab, for relief. It was there that his two sons married Moabite women. After they married, both Mahlon and Kilion, along with Elimelech, died. Naomi concludes that the land of Moab has done enough damage to her family, and she decides to go back to Bethlehem. She urges her two daughters-in-law to stay in Moab and remarry, but Ruth chooses to follow Naomi to Bethlehem. In fact, her response is one of the most beautiful and loving passages in the Scriptures. "Wherever you go, I will go; wherever you live, I will live. Your people will be my people, and your God will be my God." (Ruth 1:16)

Ruth and Naomi make it back to Bethlehem and begin scraping together a living. Ruth contributes by gleaning in the local fields. One of the provisions God made for the poor among his people was a practice that when a field was harvested you left a little margin on the borders of the field, and you didn't pick up any crop that fell to the ground. These were to be left for anyone willing to come out and harvest them for themselves.

Ruth ended up in the field of a man named Boaz. Boaz had a thing for Ruth. He was attracted to the way she cared for her mother-in-law, and he instructed his men to leave a little extra behind for her. When Ruth returned home that evening, she relayed what had happened and the kindness that the owner of the field had shown her. Naomi asked who the man was, and Ruth replied, Boaz. Naomi was so excited because this was one of their closest relatives.

Provisions were made in the Law for the closest relative to fill the role of Kinsman Redeemer. This was a relative who could deliver or rescue property or people. He could act on behalf of a relative in need, whether it be a false charge or a murder. The needs that Kinsman Redeemers usually filled were those that were created by the death of someone. The Kinsman Redeemer had the responsibility or privilege, depending on their perspective, of providing for widows. The Kinsman Redeemer is another picture of the Savior that God is sending. God's people were waiting for the day that God would send his Kinsman Redeemer to redeem mankind from their sins.

The problem in this account is that Boaz was not the closest relative to Naomi, and therefore he did not have the first privilege to act as Kinsman Redeemer for Ruth. He would first have to check with Naomi's closest relative to see if he would pass on his responsibility to Boaz. Boaz loved Ruth and wanted to redeem her as his wife. This in itself is quite interesting. It was not a normal thing for a man to be so eager to redeem a woman like Ruth. Ruth was a foreigner, and in fact it was looked down upon to marry a foreign woman. What would make Boaz want to do this voluntarily? He certainly didn't have to take her in.

A look at Boaz's family might give us a big hint. Boaz's father was a man named Salmon, who married a woman named Rahab: Yes, the Rahab from the account yesterday. Rahab was a foreigner and a prostitute, but because of her faith, she was saved from the destruction of Jericho and was brought into the Israelite family. Boaz's father looked past the outward circumstances and into Rahab's heart. He saw true faith in his wife, just like his son Boaz saw in Ruth.

So, the story continues, and we discover that Boaz's relative passed on the right to be the Kinsman Redeemer, so Boaz was able to marry Ruth. Boaz and Ruth had a son named Obed. Obed had a son named Jesse. Jesse had eight sons; the youngest was named David, who would one day become king.

Reflection Questions

1. How did Ruth show love and loyalty to her mother-in-law, Naomi, when faced with the decision to stay in Moab or go with Naomi to Bethlehem?

2. What does the term "redeem" mean, and how does it connect to God's plan for us, as explained in the text? Can you think of examples from the story of Ruth and Boaz where the concept of redemption is evident?

3. In the story, Boaz becomes a potential Kinsman Redeemer for Ruth. What does a Kinsman Redeemer do, and how does it connect to God's plan of sending a Savior?

Christmas Connection

God's promise of a great nation and a land for Abraham's descendants was fulfilled when they entered the Promised Land. As they entered, each family was given a specific plot of land that would be theirs forever. It was a visual reminder of God's promise. Upon a man's death, the land was passed down to the sons in the family. If there was no son, it became the responsibility of the closest family member, who was known as the Kinsman Redeemer, to purchase the property to keep the land in the family. Along with the family came any female family members, such as the widow of the man, so that this Kinsman Redeemer would make sure they were cared for. It was a responsibility as well as a privilege for close family members to take this role of Kinsman Redeemer. It would cost them to do it, often requiring a financial sacrifice, but they did it because they wanted to preserve the family promise.

The Kinsman Redeemer is a picture of the Savior that God was sending. Jesus would be coming to earth to pay our debt and remove the bondage of sin.

David and Goliath

David was described by God as a man after his own heart. This did not mean that David lived a perfect life. In fact, David was a major-league sinner; he committed adultery and then murdered a man to try and cover it up. One would think that with this on his resume, there is no way that "man after God's own heart" would be a phrase used to describe him. Yet it did. Not only that, but David is key in revealing God's plan of redemption.

Despite David's mistakes, he was a man of incredible faith. We are introduced to this aspect of his life very early on. David was sent one day by his father Jesse to check on his older brothers who were serving in the army. They were under the command of Saul, the first king of Israel, and were on the front lines of a battle against the Philistines. The Israelites were constantly defending the boarders of the land God had promised them through their ancestor Abraham.

As David arrived at the front line to bring his brothers supplies from home, the nine-foot-tall Philistine champion, Goliath, began to shout:

"Why are you all coming out to fight?" he
called. "I am the Philistine champion, but you
are only the servants of Saul. Choose one man
to come down here and fight me! If he kills
me, then we will be your slaves. But if I kill
him, you will be our slaves! I defy the armies
of Israel today! Send me a man who will fight
me!" (1 Sam 17:8-10)

This was David's lucky day. Not only did he get a day
off from watching the sheep back home, but he saw
all his older brothers, and he was also going to see
this battle settled once and for all! However, after
a short period of time, he realized that no one was
willing to step up and fight Goliath on behalf of the
Israelites. He was shocked! Wasn't anyone willing to
step up and fight?

David steps up in the midst of countless men who
are bigger than him, older than him, but full of fear.
The shepherd boy from the little town of Bethlehem is
confident he can take the giant. Not only had no one
else volunteered, but David found out that Goliath
had been making these threats for some time and that
all the Israelites, including King Saul, were terrified.

David approaches King Saul with his offer to
fight the giant. No one believes David can beat Goliath
except David. Why did this young man convey so

much confidence? What he says next goes a long way in explaining why God loved David so much:

> "I have been taking care of my father's sheep and goats," he said. "When a lion or a bear comes to steal a lamb from the flock, I go after it with a club and rescue the lamb from its mouth. If the animal turns on me, I catch it by the jaw and club it to death. I have done this to both lions and bears, and I'll do it to this pagan Philistine, too, for he has defied the armies of the living God! The Lord who rescued me from the claws of the lion and the bear will rescue me from this Philistine! (1 Sam 17:34-37)

David has faith. This faith has been growing for quite some time. He has seen God's faithfulness in the past in smaller things and believes him for big things. Big things like fighting a giant warrior armed only with a slingshot and some rocks. Spoiler alert: David defeats Goliath.

Fast-forwarding many years, David eventually becomes king. He is the greatest king Israel ever had. He was not without faults or errors, but he had a heart that was soft to the things of God and a faith that sustained him.

David was so pleasing to God that he chose to bring the coming of the Savior through his specific family line. God had promised to send a Savior through one of the twelve tribes of Israel, but now he was getting more specific. The Savior would be coming through the royal line of David. The prophet Isaiah further communicates God's plan:

> Out of the stump of David's family will grow a shoot—yes, a new Branch bearing fruit from the old root. And the Spirit of the Lord will rest on him—the Spirit of wisdom and understanding, the Spirit of counsel and might, the Spirit of knowledge and the fear of the Lord. . . . In that day the heir to David's throne will be a banner of salvation to all the world. The nations will rally to him, and the land where he lives will be a glorious place. In that day the Lord will reach out his hand a second time to bring back the remnant of his people—those who remain in Assyria and northern Egypt; in southern Egypt, Ethiopia, and Elam; in Babylonia, Hamath, and all the distant coastlands. (Isa 11:1-2, 10-11)

This is a prophecy about the coming Savior and the picture is getting clearer now. He will be of royal blood—the Messiah. God is sending a Savior.

Reflection Questions

1. What do you think gave David the confidence to face Goliath, even though everyone else was afraid? Can you think of a time when you had to face a big challenge or obstacle, and how did you find the courage to confront it?

2. Why do you think God chose David, despite his mistakes, to be a key figure in his plan of redemption? What qualities or characteristics did David have that made him special in God's eyes?

3. How does David's story show us that having faith in God can help us overcome difficult situations? Can you think of any ways that you can build your own faith, like David did, by remembering times when God has been faithful in the past?

Christmas Connection

David is a major part of God's rescue plan. God is sending the Savior, Jesus, directly through the royal line of David. Jesus would be a king, but not the type of king we are used to. His kingdom will last forever.

Signs of the Coming Savior

The Israelites were God's chosen people but, just like most people today, they struggled with consistency. There were seasons where the Israelites followed God's commands and worshiped at the temple; but there were also seasons where they ignored God and actually began worshiping the pagan idols of the surrounding nations.

The people almost always mirrored the king's conduct, following the same pattern. If the king showed reverence to God, the people did too. Conversely, if the king worshipped other gods, the people followed suit. God sent his prophets to warn the people of their wicked ways and of God's desire for them to turn back to him. Sometimes they would listen; other times they would not. Eventually the messages brought by the prophets would come with warnings. If the Israelites did not turn back to God, there would be consequences. God would allow their neighbors to take them into captivity as they once were in Egypt.

The prophets also brought messages of hope. God had not forgotten his promises. He was still sending a Savior. These messages were called prophecies—a message from God about future events. These messages gave the people some specific things to look for in the coming Messiah that God was sending.

Isaiah was one of these prophets that God used to reveal more details about the coming Savior. "[T]he Lord himself will give you the sign. Look! The virgin will conceive a child! She will give birth to a son and will call him Immanuel (which means 'God is with us')." (Isa 7:14)

The question that people were asking was, "how long must we wait?" The promise God had made to Abraham was over a thousand years old by this point, the plan he foreshadowed in the exodus from Egypt, the promise that every ritual and sacrifice in the temple pointed to. How much longer? When will we know your plan has started?

The Messiah will be born of a virgin. Now that's something unique and miraculous. When a virgin gives birth there should be no doubt that God's plan has started. God also reveals to Isaiah some other things to look for:

> Say to those with fearful hearts, "Be strong, and do not fear, for your God is coming to destroy your enemies. He is coming to save you." And when he comes, he will open the

eyes of the blind and unplug the ears of the deaf. The lame will leap like a deer, and those who cannot speak will sing for joy! (Isa 35:4-6)

The blind will see, the deaf will hear, and the lame will walk. Other signs that God's Savior, the Messiah, is here.

God did not want his people to miss the coming of the Savior. He would be a descendent of David, born of a virgin, make the blind see, make the deaf hear, and make the lame walk. We are starting to form a pretty good profile. It's not complete yet, there are still more prophets, with more words from God to come.

Reflection Question

1.   Why did God send prophets like Isaiah, and what were the messages these prophets delivered to the people? How did these messages help the people know about the coming Savior?

2.   What were some specific signs or miracles that the people were told to look for to recognize the coming Messiah? How do you think these signs would have reassured the people about God's plan?

Christmas Connection

God did not want his people to miss the arrival of the Savior. He began giving them signs so they would recognize what was happening. When these signs and predictions began to come true, the countdown was over, Jesus was here.

The Exile

After the time of King David and his son, King Solomon, the nation of Israel was in decline. The kingdom split into two parts after Solomon's reign; the Northern Kingdom, which retained the name Israel and had ten tribes, and the Southern Kingdom, called Judah, which consisted of the tribes of Judah and Benjamin. Judah retained the royal lineage of King David who was from that tribe.

The Northern Kingdom further distanced themselves from God by worshiping the local pagan idol named Baal. After many warnings from the prophets, God allowed foreign nations to conquer them. Those who were not taken as slaves remained behind and intermarried with their foreign captors. They eventually became identified as the Samaritans who never again lived as free people, but continually under foreign control.

Judah, although more faithful to the worship of God than the Northern Kingdom, still did not live up to the covenant God had made with his people. They too were eventually conquered by a foreign nation, the Babylonian empire. As they headed into captivity, God, through his prophet Jeremiah, gave them hope:

> This is what the Lord says: "You will be in Babylon for seventy years. But then I will come and do for you all the good things I have promised, and I will bring you home again. For I know the plans I have for you," says the Lord. "They are plans for good and not for disaster, to give you a future and hope. In those days when you pray, I will listen. If you look for me wholeheartedly, you will find me. I will be found by you," says the Lord. "I will end your captivity and restore your fortunes. I will gather you out of the nations where I sent you and will bring you home again to your own land." (Jer 29:10-14)

God never forgets his promises. He was going to send the Savior through the tribe of Judah. One of David's descendants would be the promised Messiah. In order for this to happen, God would once again have to rescue his people from exile—Another picture of what God is doing for all mankind.

Just to make sure you get the significance of what is happening here, let's talk a minute about what it means to be taken into exile. This process has been historically a one-way trip. When a conquering nation takes over a region, their goal is to expand their nation. They want one uniform country. Local customs, religion, and identity are all erased, and the reigning culture is indoctrinated into everyone. A conquering king had no time for rebels or people holding on to the past. Either you went with the program and assimilated, or you were eliminated.

Kingdoms, however, don't last forever. In fact, once you conquer a land, you have to hold on tight because it is just a matter of time before someone else wants to take it from you. New kingdoms conquered old kingdoms and that is the way it went. Never has a kingdom chosen to take a conquered people and give them everything back: land, culture, identity, or religion. It just didn't happen.

In the above passage from Jeremiah, God promises the miraculous. He would bring his people back out into their own land. He would somehow protect their identity and culture, if they would just remain faithful.

This event also demonstrates God's justice. He could no longer look on and ignore his people's rebellion and disobedience. God loved his people enough to discipline them. God is our loving father. He keeps his promise but loves us enough to correct us when needed.

The house of David will survive because God made a promise. His people, even through trials and incredibly difficult circumstances, await the coming of their true king—the Messiah—the Savior.

Reflection Questions

1. What do you think it means for God to have a plan for his people, even when they face difficult times, like exile? How does the promise God made to the Israelites in Babylon give them hope for the future, even though they were going through a challenging situation?

2. Why do you think it was important for the Israelites to remain faithful to God even during their exile in Babylon? How does this show the importance of holding onto one's identity and faith, even in difficult circumstances?

Christmas Connection

The Kingdom of Israel had broken in two. The Northern Kingdom kept the name Israel, and the Southern Kingdom was called Judah. The promise recorded in Jeremiah was written specifically to Judah. This is significant because Judah had the royal line of David. God promised that the Savior would come from that family. They had to survive the invasion. People from this family had to live on because God made a promise, and he always keeps his promises. Jesus would be born of the tribe of Judah, who would eventually return from exile, just as God promised.

A New Covenant

God's covenant agreement with his people, the Israelites, was always meant to be temporary. God clearly defined his boundaries, set expectations of what would happen if someone stepped out of those boundaries, and established steps to take in order to receive forgiveness. However, all this was just a shadow of the fulfillment of his promise to send a Savior. The Savior would provide the ultimate payment for mankind's sin.

This picture is becoming even clearer as God is sending messages of hope through his prophets to his people in exile:

> "The day is coming," says the Lord, "when I will make a new covenant with the people of Israel and Judah. This covenant will not be like the one I made with their ancestors when I took them by the hand and brought them out of the land of Egypt. They broke that covenant, though I loved them as a husband loves his wife," says the Lord. "But this is the new covenant I will make with the people of

Israel after those days," says the Lord. "I will put my instructions deep within them, and I will write them on their hearts. I will be their God, and they will be my people. And they will not need to teach their neighbors, nor will they need to teach their relatives, saying, 'You should know the Lord.' For everyone, from the least to the greatest, will know me already," says the Lord. "And I will forgive their wickedness, and I will never again remember their sins." (Jer 31:31-34)

From this message we know that the forgiveness of sin is still the central issue. God's perfect sense of justice does not change. Sin cannot be ignored. However, this is a completely different type of arrangement. This new covenant would not be written on stone tablets and placed in the temple; it would be written on the hearts of man. What could this be referring to?

What does it mean that God's instructions would be deep within them? Fortunately, we can answer this because we have the privilege of reading ahead in God's redemption story. When God sent the Messiah, the Savior—he doesn't stay on earth forever. He comes to complete his mission of paying the penalty of mankind's sin and then returns to heaven. However, God's Holy Spirit is promised upon his departure to all his followers. The Holy Spirit will live inside each believer, guiding and directing them as they seek to follow God and mature in their relationship with him.

The execution of God's plan, which began on Christmas Day, is being revealed and unveiled hundreds of years in advance. It is a message that gave hope to the hopeless. A people separated from their homeland, in exile, were promised a return, just like all of mankind is promised a return to God, through the Savior.

Reflection Questions

1. Why did God decide to make a new covenant with the people of Israel and Judah, and how is it different from the old one? What promise did God make in this new covenant?

2. In Jeremiah's message, it says that God will write his instructions on the hearts of the people. What do you think this means, and why is it important?

3. How does the Holy Spirit fit into God's plan, especially when the Savior, Jesus, completes his mission on Earth? What role does the Holy Spirit play in helping people follow God and grow in their relationship with him?

Christmas Connection

Jesus will be the final sacrifice that will ever need to be made for sin. Jesus will pay the penalty for all sin. God's new covenant with man is an internal one. The old covenant was written on stone, but this new covenant is written on our hearts.

As we count down to Christmas, we are counting down to the fulfillment of the old covenant, not the cancellation of it. When Jesus arrives, God's promises will be fulfilled.

Return from the Exile

In the first year of King Cyrus of Persia, the Lord fulfilled the prophecy he had given through Jeremiah. He stirred the heart of Cyrus to put this proclamation in writing and to send it throughout his kingdom:

This is what King Cyrus of Persia says: "The Lord, the God of heaven, has given me all the kingdoms of the earth. He has appointed me to build him a Temple at Jerusalem, which is in Judah. Any of you who are his people may go to Jerusalem in Judah to rebuild this Temple of the Lord, the God of Israel, who lives in Jerusalem. And may your God be with you! Wherever this Jewish remnant is found, let their neighbors contribute toward their expenses by giving them silver and gold, supplies for the journey, and livestock, as well as a voluntary offering for the Temple of God in Jerusalem." (Ezra 1:1-4)

The exiles were returning! God's promise was once again kept. The promise that was given to Abraham about a land, a nation, and a savior was coming closer to completion.

God demonstrated once again his desire to set his people free from the bonds of captivity just as he would free all mankind from the captivity of sin. But the exiles didn't return all together. We see several waves return over the years as Jerusalem was rebuilt from the destruction that took place when the Babylonians sacked the town.

As they returned, the first order of business was to get the temple back in operation. The temple was the lifeline between the people and God. It was the center of worship and the dwelling place of God. As the temple was being rebuilt, God sent Ezra to begin teaching the people God's law once again. God's covenant was still in place, but the people needed to be reminded of its actual teachings. They had been gone for seventy years. Almost two generations had passed. During this time, God's law had gone from being taught by the priests in the temple to stories being told in their homes in this foreign land. Much had been forgotten and some had been distorted. Ezra brought the people back to the correct teachings of God. Part of this teaching was the promise of the Messiah. There was hope still to come!

Although the geographical exile was over, God's people were not yet free. They were given back their religion and culture, but they were still governed by the Persian Empire.

Tributes, taxes, and foreign governors were part of their daily life.

Over the centuries, the empire in control would change from the Persians to the Greeks, and then to the Romans. Each proceeding ruler attempted to stomp out this small band of rebels who would not adapt to the foreign customs but clung to the worship of their one God with the unpronounceable name: "I Am." They held out hope that God was still sending the Savior, the Messiah. The one who would be their ultimate rescue from exile.

Reflection Questions

1. How do you think the return of the exiles to Jerusalem from Babylon impacted their faith in God?

2. Why was it important for them to rebuild the temple, and how did it symbolize their restoration and connection with God?

3. How did Ezra's role in teaching God's law help to guide the people back to their spiritual roots and identity? How can we apply the lessons learned from the return of the exiles to our own lives when we face challenges or setbacks?

Christmas Connection

For God's promises about the coming Savior to come true, his people needed to be back in their land. God was sending the Savior, and the people needed to be home for it to happen.

Location Bethlehem

God had brought his people out of exile back into his promised land, but they were still under foreign control. God continued to encourage his people through the prophets by giving them reminders and signs to look for in the coming Messiah.

In all, God gave about sixty specific prophesies about the coming Messiah. The combination of all of these predications created a picture of the coming Savior that would be hard to miss. In fact, statisticians calculated the probability of just eight of the prophecies coming true for a random individual. That probability, calculated in the book *Science Speaks*, by Peter Stoner and Robert Newman, was $1:10^{17}$. In longhand form, that is 1:100,000,000,000,000,000. In the book, they use an illustration to bring this to life. It would be like taking the state of Texas and filling it two feet deep with silver dollars. One would then mark one of the silver dollars and randomly mix it into the pile. The probability of a person fulfilling eight predictions about their life is the same as the probability of picking out that marked silver dollar.

The amazing thing is that the Messiah didn't have eight prophesies about his life, there were about sixty. The probabilities at that point are enormous. The arrival of the Savior was so important; God did not want us to miss it. He also knew that others would come along and try to lead people astray by claiming to be the Messiah.

These prophesies were not things that someone could intentionally make happen either. You cannot choose your ancestors or your mother, and you cannot choose how you will die. You certainly cannot choose where you will be born.

The prophet Micah gave one of the most known prophesies about the coming Messiah. Micah revealed the town where the Messiah would be born: "But you, O Bethlehem Ephrathah, are only a small village among all the people of Judah. Yet a ruler of Israel, whose origins are in the distant past, will come from you on my behalf." (Mic 5:2) The Savior, the Messiah would be born in Bethlehem.

God provided hope to his people through the prophets. He provided words of encouragement, words of correction, words of hope, and words of expectation—until it stopped. Malachi was the last of the prophets, the last of God's messengers. After Malachi, God was silent.

There were four hundred years of silence. Four hundred years of clinging on to God's promise of the Messiah. Four hundred years of hoping for the promised Savior. Four hundred years is a long time to wait in silence.

Reflection Questions

1. Why did God give so many prophecies about the coming Messiah, and what is the significance of these predictions having such a low probability of coming true by chance?

2. How did the prophet Micah contribute to the fulfillment of God's plan by specifying the town where the Messiah would be born? Why do you think it was important for God to provide specific details, like the birthplace of the Savior?

3. After the prophet Malachi, the text mentions four hundred years of silence from God. How do you think the people during that time felt? How might this have affected their hope for the promised Savior?

Christmas Connection

God has now given the birthplace of the Savior—Bethlehem, the hometown of King David.

John the Baptist

As the Old Testament concludes, God spoke through one last prophet, Malachi. In this short book, a prophecy is given about the promised Messiah. To be more specific, a prophecy is given about someone who will come right before the Messiah to prepare the way for him.

> "Look! I am sending my messenger, and he will prepare the way before me. Then the Lord you are seeking will suddenly come to his Temple. The messenger of the covenant, whom you look for so eagerly, is surely coming," says the Lord of Heaven's Armies. (Mal 3:1)

This verse brings a little more clarity to another passage from Isaiah, written about two hundred years earlier, before the exile: "Listen! It's the voice of someone shouting, 'Clear the way through the wilderness for the Lord! Make a straight highway through the wasteland for our God.'" (Isa 40:3)

After Malachi gave his prophesy, God was then silent for over four hundred years. This does not mean that God stopped loving his people. It also did not mean that his people stopped loving him. There was simply nothing more to say. God had made his promise. God had reinforced his promise. God demonstrated over and over his commitment to that promise. He told his people what to look for in the coming Messiah. Even with all this, God's love for man was demonstrated in that he would send a messenger to come right before the Messiah to prepare the way. He did not want anyone to miss the Savior.

Zechariah was a priest during the reign of King Herod and was married to a woman named Elizabeth. This couple was incredibly Godly—and incredibly old. Their one regret in life was that they were never able to have any children. Now, in their old age, they were resigned to the fact that this would not change and that they would never get to experience this blessing from God, despite their prayers.

The Gospel of Luke records an incredible event that took place in the temple one day while Zachariah was working. The angel Gabriel paid him a visit:

> While Zechariah was in the sanctuary, an angel of the Lord appeared to him, standing to the right of the incense altar. Zechariah was shaken and overwhelmed with fear when he saw him. But the angel said, "Don't be

afraid, Zechariah! God has heard your prayer. Your wife, Elizabeth, will give you a son, and you are to name him John. You will have great joy and gladness, and many will rejoice at his birth, for he will be great in the eyes of the Lord. He must never touch wine or other alcoholic drinks. He will be filled with the Holy Spirit, even before his birth. And he will turn many Israelites to the Lord their God. He will be a man with the spirit and power of Elijah. He will prepare the people for the coming of the Lord. He will turn the hearts of the fathers to their children, and he will cause those who are rebellious to accept the wisdom of the godly." (Luke 1:11-17)

Zachariah had a hard time believing the angel at first (for obvious reasons); because of this, his voice was taken away until John was born. However, after this initial stumble, Zachariah and his wife did exactly as the angel Gabriel commanded. They named their son John and set him apart for the Lord's work from birth.

John grew into a great man. He preached repentance to the people, in preparation for the coming of the Messiah. To repent means to turn away or reject something. John specifically preached repentance or turning away from one's sin. The Messiah was coming, and John would spend his life letting everyone know that God's promises were about to come true. The centuries of waiting were over. God's Savior was on his way!

Reflection Questions

1. Today's devotional records two long waits, four hundred silent years and Zachariah and Elizabeth's wait for a child. What is the longest wait you have ever had and how did you make it through?

2. In what ways did John the Baptist fulfill the prophecies given about him in the Old Testament, particularly those from Malachi and Isaiah?

3. How did John's ministry pave the way for Jesus' own ministry and the fulfillment of God's promises to his people?

Christmas Connection

John the Baptist is the prophet predicted in the Old Testament that would come and prepare the way for the Messiah. The arrival of John the Baptist signals the coming of the Savior, Jesus!

DECEMBER 21

An Angel Visits Mary

> In the sixth month of Elizabeth's pregnancy, God sent the angel Gabriel to Nazareth, a village in Galilee, to a virgin named Mary. She was engaged to be married to a man named Joseph, a descendant of King David. Gabriel appeared to her and said, "Greetings, favored woman! The Lord is with you!" (Luke 1:26-28)

These verses in the beginning of the Gospel of Luke quickly begin to bring together thousands of years of expectation and promises. Gabriel continues to reveal to Mary what is about to happen: she will have a child even though she is a virgin. This will not be a child by natural means, but by supernatural ones. God was stepping into human history. All the promises he has made to his people about the coming Messiah will be fulfilled through the birth of this child.

For the first time, this child is given a personal name. Many different titles had been attached to his arrival through the prophets: Messiah, Savior, Son of God, Son of Man, Son of the Most High, Emmanuel—but now the name Jesus is revealed.

Jesus, the Son of God, was coming to earth to rescue mankind from their sins. John the Baptist was preparing the way for his arrival and now we know his earthly mother is a young girl named Mary.

What was so special about Mary? Why did God choose her? The passage simply says that she had found favor with God. Now we can assume that this had something to do with her good character and devotion to God. These things would obviously be pleasing to God and cause her to find favor with him. More than likely, however, there were other young girls who were devout and obedient. Many times, in Scripture, when God singles someone out for their character, the point is usually made that God found only this one person of good character, or explicitly states that their character highly surpassed that of their peers. I don't think that this is the case here. I believe what made Mary special and caused God to choose her can be found in her reaction to the news. It is one of simple obedience.

Mary's life was about to get very complicated. She was going to have to tell her fiancé that she was pregnant, hoping that he would believe her when she relayed her account of the angel's visit. She was also going to have to endure the whispers from the community, as they more than likely would judge her as her belly began to grow with child. While these were temporary inconveniences, she still faced the pressure of raising a child who was the Savior of the world, God in the flesh. The One whom she worshipped would now be under her care during his vulnerable childhood. What if she made mistakes? What if she did something wrong?

Mary showed amazing faith in God. Even though she didn't have all the details and didn't know how things would unfold, she believed that God was in control. If God believed in her to handle this responsibility, Mary felt she could trust him with all the specific plans and challenges that would come her way.

Mary's quick obedience might lead one to believe that she didn't quite understand the implications of what was happening. As we continue to read on in the Gospel of Luke, we find recorded, Mary's Song, and as we read, it is apparent that she did understand. It is her beautiful response to all that is happening through her. It is an incredible balance of humility and the significance of what is unfolding:

> "Oh, how my soul praises the Lord.
> How my spirit rejoices in God my Savior!
> For he took notice of his lowly servant girl,
>   and from now on all generations will
>   call me blessed.
> For the Mighty One is holy,

and he has done great things for me.
He shows mercy from generation to
	generation to all who fear him.
His mighty arm has done tremendous things!
He has scattered the proud and haughty ones.
He has brought down princes from
	their thrones and exalted the humble.
He has filled the hungry with good things
	and sent the rich away with empty hands.
He has helped his servant Israel
	and remembered to be merciful.
For he made this promise to our ancestors,
	to Abraham and his children forever."
(Luke 1:46-55)

Reflection Questions

1. Why did God choose Mary for such an important role, and what qualities do you think made her special?

2. How do you think Mary felt when she learned about the challenges she would face, such as telling her fiancé and enduring judgment from the community? How did her faith in God help her navigate these difficulties?

3. In Mary's Song (Luke 1:46-55), what emotions and thoughts does Mary express? How does her response show a balance of humility and an understanding of the significance of the events unfolding in her life?

Christmas Connection

The prophecies are being fulfilled with the arrival of Jesus. A virgin will give birth to the Savior, and he will be born of the line of David. Mary is an unmarried descendant of King David. God's promises are coming true, and we will see all the others fulfilled through the birth and life of Jesus.

The Honorable Joseph

We do not know a lot of about Joseph, Jesus' earthly father. However, what we do know is that he was an incredibly honorable man.

Mary eventually must tell her fiancé about her pregnancy. One could probably imagine how that conversation went.

Mary:"Joseph, you need to sit down for this.
    I am pregnant."
Joseph: *feels heartbroken*
Mary:"But it's not what you think."
Joseph:"Really, how so?"
Mary:"An angel visited me and told me that I am
    carrying the Messiah. I am pregnant by the
    Holy Spirit."
Joseph:*feels confused*
Mary:"You believe me, right?"
Joseph:*feels betrayed*

Of course we don't know exactly how the conversation went. However, one thing is absolutely apparent from the Gospel of Matthew, Joseph doesn't believe Mary.

True character is revealed in the most difficult of circumstances. It's easy to have integrity and good character when everything is going your way and life is following your preplanned expectations. However, when difficulties arise, when expectations are not met, when disappointments come your way, the way one reacts in those situations is the real indication of one's heart. As we look at Joseph's response to Mary's pregnancy, we get an incredible snapshot of the type of man Joseph really is—honorable.

During the first century, in this culture and community, Joseph would have been completely within his rights to make an example of his presumably unfaithful fiancé. He could have had her severely punished and received a sense of justice for the betrayal he believed he was enduring. However, Joseph chose a different path. He didn't act quickly or react emotionally to the news. Joseph went away to consider his options. We are told that the option he was leaning toward was the most compassionate one. He would quietly break off the engagement with Mary and move on without a public scene.

While he thought about these things, Joseph had a dream. This was not just a regular dream; it was a vision from God. In Matthew we read what happens as Joseph is grappling with this situation:

As he considered this, an angel of the Lord appeared to him in a dream. "Joseph, son of David," the angel said, "do not be afraid to take Mary as your wife. For the child within her was conceived by the Holy Spirit. And she will have a son, and you are to name him Jesus,[a] for he will save his people from their sins."(Matt 1:20-21)

Mary's story was confirmed. God was at work here. Jesus, the Messiah, was going to be born. This was the Savior they had been waiting for. This was the fulfillment of God's plan to conquer sin.

Joseph awoke and did exactly as the angel commanded him to, taking Mary as his wife.

Reflection Questions

1. How do you think Joseph felt when Mary first told him about her pregnancy? What emotions might he have experienced, and why might he have found it difficult to believe her explanation?

2. How did Joseph's reaction demonstrate his character and honor?

3. When Joseph received a message from God in a dream, how do you think he felt? What might have been going through his mind as he heard the angel's words?

4. How did Joseph's obedience to the angel's command contribute to the fulfillment of God's plan for Jesus as the Savior?

Christmas Connection

God handpicked his earthly parents. What an honor to be chosen by God for such a special task. God used Joseph to fulfill the role of Jesus' earthly father.

The Journey to Bethlehem

There have always been several motivating factors when it comes to leaders expanding their territories and conquering new lands: security, power, and financial gains. Taxes and tributes have been imposed on conquered nations since the time when nations first began conquering other nations. Taxes are most often calculated and collected based on population. Therefore, to set the amount of taxes a region would be expected to pay, one needed to conduct an accurate census. This is exactly what Caesar Augustus mandated during Mary's pregnancy.

For the census to be conducted with some type of order, each male was required to travel to his family's ancestral land to register. Since Joseph was a descendant of King David, he was required to travel from his current home in Nazareth to the city of Bethlehem.

In ordinary circumstances, this journey could have been something the newly married couple looked forward to. And even though going to Bethlehem wasn't a choice but something they had to do, why not try to enjoy it? Traveling to your family's hometown, spending time with relatives, and exploring new places—this trip could have been full of adventure and fun. However, things can be different when you're pregnant and about to have a baby. For this couple, the journey had misery written all over it.

When a woman is nine months pregnant, driving in the car is not a pleasant experience. When a woman is nine months pregnant, traveling over sixty miles by foot or on the back of a donkey is characterized by words that cannot be published in a Christmas book. To top it off, when Mary and Joseph arrive in Bethlehem, all the rooms are filled. Imagine: Joseph and his pregnant wife are the last to arrive and there is no place reserved for them to rest.

An innkeeper took pity on them and offered up a stable for them to stay in because it was apparent that Mary would be giving birth very soon. It was in these very humble beginnings that God chose to come to earth.

God uses all kinds of people to bring about his plans. God had promised that he would send a Savior and that he would be born of the line of David. He was fulfilling this prophesy through Joseph and Mary who were both descendants of the ancient royal line. He also gave his people a sign that this child would be born in Bethlehem. God used Caesar's decree to bring Mary and Joseph from Nazareth to Bethlehem for Jesus' birth.

Reflection Questions

1. Why did Caesar Augustus order a census, and how did it lead to Mary and Joseph's journey to Bethlehem?

2. What challenges do you think Mary and Joseph faced during their journey to Bethlehem, especially considering Mary's pregnancy?

3. Why do you think God chose a humble setting like a stable for the birth of Jesus?

Christmas Connection

Joseph and Mary lived in Nazareth. God told his people that the Savior would be born in Bethlehem. Isn't it amazing how God always makes his promises come true—every last detail!

Christmas Eve—The Shepherds

On the night that Jesus was born, events began to occur that signaled the Savior was not going to fit everyone's expectations. God's people were awaiting their final rescue from exile. Although they were in the promised land, they were still under Roman control and authority. Surely, if God was going to save them, he would deal with the Romans first.

A new king is what they were looking for. I mean, the Savior *was* coming from the line of David. They *were* in desperate need of a real leader among them. They were expecting that God was going to send the Messiah to set them free from the Romans and lead them back into a proper relationship with God.

God was doing something much more profound through Jesus. He was on a mission to conquer sin and death. Empires and rulers came and went. The real enemy of God's people, and all people, was sin, which separated them from him. Jesus would not arrive at a palace or in the home of a powerful well-connected family. His birth would not be met by royals and dignitaries from within the Israelite community. No official announcements would be sent out ushering in the birth of this new king.

Jesus was born into a very normal family under very abnormal circumstances. Jesus was born in a stable and placed in a manger; a feeding trough for animals was his first bed. Beginnings do not get humbler than this. The announcement of his birth went out to the local shepherds working in the fields that night:

> That night there were shepherds staying in the fields nearby, guarding their flocks of sheep. Suddenly, an angel of the Lord appeared among them, and the radiance of the Lord's glory surrounded them. They were terrified, but the angel reassured them. "Don't be afraid!" he said. "I bring you good news that will bring great joy to all people. The Savior—yes, the Messiah, the Lord—has been born today in Bethlehem, the city of David! And you will recognize him by this sign: You will find a baby wrapped snugly in strips of cloth, lying in a manger."
>
> Suddenly, the angel was joined by a vast host of others—the armies of heaven—praising God and saying,
>
> "Glory to God in highest heaven, and peace on earth to those with whom God is pleased." (Luke 2:8-14)

God didn't hold back on the announcement. Angels were singing by the multitudes, praising God, and announcing the birth of Jesus. It was the audience that was unusual. God chose to reveal this amazing announcement to normal, everyday people. In fact, some might make the argument that these shepherds were actually the lowest class of people. Shepherds were not highly regarded—so much so that their testimony was typically not taken as fact if needed for court. Yet here we have God making the most important announcement in the history of the world to these men.

As we have seen through this countdown to Christmas journey, these are the types of people God most often uses. We continue to see this through the life of Jesus. As he begins teaching the people about the kingdom of God and proving that he is the Messiah through miracles, it is the poor and working-class that flock to Jesus. They are able to trust and have faith in him because they recognize their own faults.

The shepherds in the field have no problem believing what they see and immediately seek out the newly-born Savior. They arrive at the stable and find Jesus just as the angels had described. This snapshot of man's first encounter with the Savior echoes those that man will experience throughout the life of Jesus.

Even more fascinating, it echoes encounters with him that people still experience today. Meeting Jesus was so impactful that they could not keep the news to themselves; they came away changed. They had to talk about this encounter with everyone they came across and interacted with. One cannot have an encounter with Jesus and walk away the same.

Jesus has arrived. God's promise is fulfilled. Mankind will be rescued from exile. Not from exile to a foreign land or distant emperor, but an exile from God caused by sin. Jesus, God in the flesh, came to rescue mankind from their sin. He would do this by paying the penalty for sin that we could not pay ourselves. Jesus gave his life for us. He died as a final sacrifice to pay the penalty for man's sin.

This gift of forgiveness is not for the spiritual elite. It's not for those who have their act together and always seem to say the right thing and do the right thing. This gift of forgiveness is available to anyone who is able to recognize his or her failures and shortcomings and turn to him. Mankind has to admit their sin and repent. As one turns from their sin, there is a Savior waiting with arms wide open to forgive anyone who will put their faith in him.

Reflection Questions

1. Why do you think God chose to announce the birth of Jesus to shepherds, people who were not highly regarded in society at that time? How might this choice reflect God's character and his message about who Jesus came to save?

2. After encountering Jesus, the shepherds couldn't keep the news to themselves; they shared it with everyone they met. Why do you think meeting Jesus had such a profound impact on them? What does their response to meeting Jesus teach us about sharing the good news with others?

Christmas Connection

God's plan is so much bigger than setting people free from a dictator or tyrant. God is going to save us from sin itself. Jesus the Savior is here!

DECEMBER 25

Christmas Day

Christmas Day has finally arrived. Today we celebrate the birth of Jesus through a variety of traditions. Some of those traditions are religious in nature, while others are adapted from our culture. Some traditions are a hybrid of both religious and cultural practices.

One of the oldest Christmas traditions is giving gifts. Even though we can't pinpoint its exact beginnings, we do know that special visitors gave gifts to Jesus when he was born. Wise men from the East came to see the newborn King of the Jews.

These wise men knew about Jesus' arrival because they studied the stars. This knowledge likely came from the influence the Israelites had on the Babylonian and Persian empires during their captivity. In the Scriptures, it's clear that Daniel and other talented Jewish men served foreign kings during their captivity. Daniel and his peers became the wise men advising the kings. Being part of this group, they would naturally share their expectations about God sending the Messiah. This gave them the opportunity to discuss the signs and prophecies they anticipated for the arrival of the King of the Jews.

The wise men from the East did not have the complete story when they arrived because they showed up in Jerusalem at the palace of Herod looking for the new heir. One can only assume that a newborn king would be at the palace.

There wasn't a baby at the palace, and when the wise men shared their news with Herod, he got worried. Herod kept his concerns hidden and called for religious scholars to learn more about where they should find the coming Messiah. The scholars quickly told them to look in Bethlehem, as the prophets had predicted. Herod sent the wise men on their way with instructions to report back to him so that he too might go and make a special visit to the newborn king.

As the wise men arrived at the house where Jesus lay, they immediately fell down and worshiped Jesus. They presented gifts of gold, frankincense, and myrrh.

Reflection Questions

1. Why is giving gifts a common tradition during Christmas, and what do you think it represents or symbolizes in celebrating Jesus' birth?

2. How did the wise men know about Jesus, and what did they bring as gifts?

3. When the wise men arrived in Jerusalem, they assumed the newborn king would be at the palace. Why do you think they thought this, and how did their journey change when they didn't find the baby there?

Christmas Connection

The promise God made to Abraham was that if Abraham had the faith to trust him, God would give him a land and a great nation, and the whole world would be blessed through them. That blessing was Jesus. He came for the benefit of the whole world. At his birth, his impact was already being felt beyond the boundaries of Judaea. The wise men traveled from a distant place to honor the newborn king. He wasn't the kind of king they had anticipated, but from their responses, we can see that they discovered that he was something much greater. The wise men recognized the newborn king, King Jesus. He had come to save the whole world!

FOCOLARE MEDIA

Enkindling the Spirit of Unity

The New City Press book you are holding in your hands is one of the many resources produced by Focolare Media, which is a ministry of the Focolare Movement in North America. The Focolare is a worldwide community of people who feel called to bring about the realization of Jesus' prayer: "That all may be one" (see John 17:21).

Focolare Media wants to be your primary resource for connecting with people, ideas, and practices that build unity. Our mission is to provide content that empowers people to grow spiritually, improve relationships, engage in dialogue, and foster collaboration within the Church and throughout society.

Visit www.focolaremedia.com to learn more about all of New City Press's books, our award-winning magazine *Living City*, videos, podcasts, events, and free resources.

NCP
NEW CITY PRESS

www.ingramcontent.com/pod-product-compliance
Lightning Source LLC
Chambersburg PA
CBHW051727090426
42738CB00010B/2123